Original title:
The Call of the Sea Breeze

Copyright © 2025 Creative Arts Management OÜ
All rights reserved.

Author: Kieran Blackwood
ISBN HARDBACK: 978-1-80581-553-2
ISBN PAPERBACK: 978-1-80581-080-3
ISBN EBOOK: 978-1-80581-553-2

Ashore Beneath the Starlit Skies

Under the moon, we hold our flags,
While crabs play tag with our old rags.
Seagulls squawk with comedic flair,
Trying to steal our ice cream, beware!

The stars above like tiny eyes,
Watch us dance like we're in disguise.
We trip over sandcastles so grand,
While the waves giggle, "This is your land!"

Sails that Dance with Dreams

On wooden ships with sails so wide,
We set out on a foolish ride.
Fins of fish wave 'hello' and flee,
As we scream, "Look! A whale!" Then just debris!

The wind whispers jokes, oh what a tease,
As we bounce around like 'Who's got the keys?'
With every gust that blows us awry,
We start to wonder if we can fly!

Whirlwinds of Freedom and Adventure

Spin us round like tops on the sand,
We're tossed with laughter, isn't it grand?
A parrot squawks, "You call that a sail?"
As snacks fly away, oh dear, our fail!

We race the tides with shouts and cheer,
Daring the wind to list and veer.
Each splash is a giggle, a tickling tease,
While we dodge jellyfish with total unease!

The Spirit of Windswept Shores

Upon the dune, we wiggle and jig,
As the sea breeze nudges, oh, it's so big!
Sandy toes and laughter in the air,
While the tide tries to steal my favorite chair!

Out in the waves, our shouts of glee,
Join with the chorus of the chuckling sea.
We toss our hats, like confetti on waves,
Who knew fun lived in the ocean's caves?

Secrets in the Whispering Currents

A fish once wore a hat so fine,
He claimed it made him quite divine.
But every time he'd swim and shake,
It slipped and sank, oh what a break!

The crabs would chuckle as they'd play,
And tease him 'bout the hat each day.
He'd blush and puff with great dismay,
"It'll be back!" he'd always say.

Sighs of the Twilight Waters

The seagulls squawked with comic flair,
Mistook a sandwich for a chair.
They perched and took a clumsy bite,
Then flew away, it was quite the sight!

While fish beneath were plotting schemes,
To steal away the gull's lost dreams.
They danced and splashed in gleeful cheer,
"The gulls won't know, we have no fear!"

Enchantment of the Rolling Surf

A clam once opened wide to sing,
But only made a splashy thing.
His voice was more like funny gurgles,
The tide soon rolled in with subtle burbles!

Nearby a starfish tried to groove,
But ended up with quite the move.
He tripped and fell upon the sand,
His friends all laughed, it wasn't planned!

Currents of the Morning Mist

A wave decided it was bold,
And slapped a surfer; true, the gold!
But missed the chance to catch his ride,
And laughed instead, with bubbling pride!

With every push, they surfed in fun,
Like friends who race to meet the sun.
Their playful splashes filled the air,
And giggles echoed everywhere!

Lullaby of the Nautical Night

As tides hug the shore with glee,
Crabs dance jigs, so wild and free.
Stars twinkle down, a playful sight,
Whispers echo in the moonlight.

A fish forgot its swimming style,
Wobbles past with a goofy smile.
Seagulls giggle, taking flight,
While clams chant songs 'til the dawn's light.

Secrets in the Nautical Air

In a treasure chest, I found some cheese,
Sailed the ocean with the greatest ease.
But gulls conspired, stole my lunch,
Leaving me with only a crunchy bunch.

Waves whisper tales of silly fish,
Who dream of being a priceless dish.
Octopuses juggle with great flair,
While turtles giggle, without a care.

Shimmering Tides and Swaying Palms

Palm trees sway to a breezy tune,
While crabs go crabbing under the moon.
A beach ball rolls, chasing some toes,
A seagull squawks—'Oh, you're too close!'

Sandcastles crumble with a thud,
A family slips in the mud and the crud.
Laughter dances on the warm sea air,
As dolphins splash without a care.

Breath of the Surging Sea

Bubbles float up, a fizzy delight,
Fish parade, sporting new shoes quite bright.
Pirates stroll with a silly strut,
As mermaids giggle, 'Look at that nut!'

Shells are whispering jokes far and wide,
While sea turtles take them for a ride.
At sunset, laughter fills the skies,
Every wave telling tales and lies.

Mists of the Morning Coast

In the fog, the seagulls prance,
They steal your fries, then take a stance,
With feathers ruffled, they squawk and dive,
Making breakfast on the beach a jive.

The waves skip up, then run away,
While sandcastles start to sway,
A crab snaps at a passing shoe,
Who knew he fancied bright red, too?

Triptych of the Ocean's Breath

Oh, the ocean sings a silly tune,
It tickles your toes, it mocks the moon,
With splashes loud and whispers sly,
It pulls you in, then waves goodbye.

A dolphin leaps in a sparkling dance,
For a moment, you think it's true romance,
But it's just fish that really thrill,
Who knew seafood could give such a chill?

Fragrance of Distant Shores

A breeze brings scents from far-off lands,
Like fishy tacos and odd little bands,
It rustles hats into the sea,
And laughs at folks who wear them free.

Shells whisper tales of underwater glee,
While beach balls roam so wild and free,
Some kids fall down, it's quite a scene,
As laughter echoes, bright and keen.

Serenities in the Gale

The wind has jokes, it's quite a tease,
It twirls your skirt and bends the trees,
Every gust boasts of a breezy plan,
While you try to dance like a graceful swan.

Sand zooms past like a mischievous foe,
It gets in your sandwich, then steals the show,
With every laugh, the waves do cheer,
At the silly dance of summer's rear.

Portraits in the Sea's Canvas

With a hat made of fish, he took to the shore,
His trousers were netting, he needed no more.
Seagulls all laughed, as he danced in the sand,
Claiming he's best, a true sea-faring man.

Shells whispering secrets, they giggle and tease,
While crabs wear sunglasses, quite eager to please.
A dolphin's a painter, splashing colors so bright,
On canvas of waves, they create day and night.

Petals of Ocean Breezes

The wind swept in with a tickle and tease,
Sending hats flying like leaves on the breeze.
Children all giggle, chase kites in the sky,
While sandcastles wobble and tumble nearby.

A beach ball takes flight, it's a merry old sight,
Bound to the laughter, it carts off from flight.
Each wave lifts a chuckle, a frolic, a dance,
As mermaids in seashells give seaweed a glance.

The Wandering Gale's Heartbeat

The zephyr arrives with a whoosh and a whirr,
Socks off to the surf, oh, what a stir!
Breezes that giggle, they swirl all around,
Turning grown-ups to children, where joy can be found.

A parrot in shades announces grand news,
'The sand's hot as pancakes, come, take off your shoes!'
Surfboards are flying, much to our surprise,
As waves turn to laughter, beneath sunny skies.

Harmonies of Wind and Water

In the mix of the tide, a riddle takes flight,
With seahorses singing their tunes through the night.
Each splash of the surf is a note, bold and clear,
While fish play the cello, the beach is their sphere.

A starfish conductor waves arms made of glee,
As raindrops join in, dancing wild and free.
The concert of chaos, a whimsical jam,
With kelp as the curtains, just look at the clam!

Hymn of the Horizon's Edge

The waves dance and twirl with glee,
While seagulls laugh, oh so silly.
We chase the tide, what a wild spree,
With sand in our shoes, we feel quite free.

A crab named Larry plans a race,
With clumsy feet, he sets the pace.
He trips and flops, oh what a face!
We cheer and laugh, he wins by grace!

The sun goes down, the sky's bright hue,
It's bedtime now for crabs and crew.
Yet our laughter echoes, loud and true,
As we dream of shells and skies so blue.

Murmurs from the Deep Blue

The ocean's secrets, so they say,
Are whispered in the salt spray play.
We listen close, hip-hip-hooray,
As fish make jokes that steal the day.

A dolphin jumps, a leaping jest,
With flips and tricks, he's the best.
He splashes us with his ocean fest,
And we just laugh, it's our sea quest!

The jellyfish glide with goofy grace,
In a wobbly, dancing underwater race.
No one can match their squishy pace,
We cheer them on from our sunny place.

Caress of the Gentle Waves

The gentle lap, a bubbly tease,
The waves are tickling our bare knees.
We giggle loud, just like the breeze,
As sea foam plays and dances with ease.

A starfish smiles with a wink and grin,
He joins our dance, let the fun begin!
We spin around, and round we spin,
With every splash, a goofy win!

When crabs do the cha-cha on the sand,
We join them quick, isn't it grand?
With laughter ringing, oh so unplanned,
The ocean's party is simply unbanned!

Breezy Embrace of Distant Shores

A seagull swoops, in playful flight,
He steals my fries, oh what a sight!
We laugh and shout, the mood is bright,
As waves keep time in the fading light.

The wind brings melodies from afar,
With salty songs, we sing bizarre.
A crab in shades takes a ride in my car,
He's the new star, it's going to be a spar!

The beach flags wave, a silly parade,
With flip-flops flying, oh what a charade!
Under the sun, the fun never fades,
Life is a joke, and we're all unafraid!

Ocean's Whisper in Twilight

In twilight's glow, the waves do dance,
Seagulls squawk, they take a chance.
A crab winks under the moon's soft light,
Thinking it's king, what a funny sight!

The tides come in, they pull and tease,
As fish join in with silly ease.
A dog jumps, thinking he can swim,
Splashing around on a whim so grim!

Sandcastles rise, with dreams to boast,
Until a wave shows who's the host.
Each grain of sand whispers a jest,
Nature's humor, we can't contest!

So as the stars twinkle above,
The ocean laughs, sharing its love.
Making memories, both wild and free,
In the salty air, we all agree!

Tales Woven in the Breeze

The wind tells tales of ships that sway,
Bringing whispers from far away.
A fish with dreams of flying high,
Looks to the gulls as they pass by!

Shells gossip softly, in a pile,
Sharing secrets with a cheeky smile.
A pair of dolphins, up to no good,
Invite the seals for a splashing flood!

The crabs throw parties under the sun,
While waves recommend that everyone run.
But what's this? A jellyfish in disguise,
Bobbing along with wide-open eyes!

So heed the breeze and its frolicsome air,
Join the fun, let go of your care.
For beneath the sea's playful tease,
Laughter rises like the sweetest breeze!

The Ocean's Gentle Invitation

Come closer, says the ocean wide,
With a wink and a gurgle, it beckons with pride.
A wave rolls in just to tickle your toes,
Leaving behind a splash as it goes!

Eels twist and turn in a comedy show,
Wiggling and giggling with quite a glow.
The sandbar hosts a laugh-out-loud crowd,
As starfish applaud, feeling quite proud!

A sea turtle wears a silly hat,
While crabs collaborate, looking just like that.
So join in the joy, let laughter flow,
Take a dip in the antics the ocean bestows!

For when the sun sets and shadows play,
The sea will tell jokes in a merry way.
With every ripple, each bubble of glee,
You're invited to join the fun of the sea!

Risings of the Misty Horizon

Morning breaks as mist begins to rise,
The horizon giggles under brightening skies.
A fishing line meant to hook a prized catch,
Instead catches seagulls, now isn't that a match?

Bubbles pop and giggles erupt,
As fishes tease, their swim styles corrupt.
A whale listens in, with a grin so wide,
For it knows all secrets that the tides can't hide!

Shells play cards, but they can't play fair,
As the tide keeps changing, with a mischievous air.
The dolphin pulls pranks, flipping with glee,
While the silly old ocean just laughs with me!

So as the day dawns and mischief reigns,
The horizon brightens, loosens our chains.
Embrace the joy where water and sky blend,
With laughter that carries, let the fun never end!

Winds of Remembrance

A gentle gust whispers near,
Tickling my ears, oh so clear.
A fishy tale begins to reel,
As I dance with this wavy feel.

It blows past my sandwich spread,
Crumbs fly like dreams in my head.
Seagulls squawk and chase the breeze,
While I just hope for fries and cheese.

Laughter echoes, driftwood laughs,
As I juggle shells and scoff at gaffes.
Memories swirl in this salty song,
With each gust, I feel I belong.

So here, I breathe in the brine,
With wind-swept hair, I sip my wine.
Fleeting moments, carefree and light,
This coastal breeze just feels so right.

Secrets beneath the Sand

Beneath the surface, treasures hide,
Not just shells, but secrets wide!
A flip-flop lost, a funny sight,
As crabs scurry, oh, what a fright!

I dug too deep, what did I find?
A rubber duck, so well-defined.
It quacks at me with sandy glee,
A friend to share this beachy spree.

Footprints lead to nowhere fast,
Chasing waves, I'm quite the blast.
The tide's wild dance, I jump and skip,
As laughter bubbles like a soda sip.

Oh, secrets buried with the tide,
Giggles echo where dreams collide.
Each grain of sand, a chuckle retained,
In this sandy realm, hilarity's gained.

My Heart, the Wanderer

My heart's a boat with sails unfurled,
Sailing 'round this wondrous world.
It veers and dips, it spins about,
Chasing dreams without a doubt.

But then a gust, it sends me careening,
Straight into feet that are intervening.
"Excuse me!" I yell, with a laugh and a grin,
As I stumble back, trying to win.

Waves of giggles crash and play,
As my heart wanders, come what may.
Each nudge reminds me to just be free,
Dance with the wind, it's the life for me!

So, onward it goes, this silly beat,
With a flip-flop here and a sand surprise greet.
In each new port, with laughter and cheer,
My heart's a wanderer, no need for fear.

Romantic Echoes of Tidal Graces

The ocean serenades my stroll,
With lines so cheesy, it takes its toll.
A clam whispers sweet nothings, oh dear!
While I blush at the whispers I hear.

Shells signal love in the softest breeze,
Yet my hopes get dashed, like waves on the knees.
With each salty kiss, I pretend to swoon,
As crabs dance by, beneath the moon.

A seagull squawks, "Hey, don't you dare!"
Stealing my fries's in hopeless affair.
It flaps like it's mocking my silly delight,
While I chuckle and throw it a bite.

So here's to romance, both strange and whimsical,
Tidal graces make my heart lyrical.
With laughter echoing o'er dark blue seas,
I'll keep twirling between love and the breeze.

Ebbing Dreams and Flowing Wishes

Waves chuckle as they crash and spray,
A fishy joke just swam my way!
The shore holds laughter, the sea a grin,
As I chase thoughts that drift like tin.

Seagulls gossip from their lofty seat,
Pecking at crumbs of a tourist's treat.
A sandy pie I built with pride,
Ends up a feast for gulls outside!

Ebbing dreams on the shore I find,
Each ripple whispers jokes to unwind.
With each retreat, my hopes collide,
Finding treasures where joy can hide!

Like wishes in bubbles, they float away,
Turning to giggles with each play.
The ocean sings with a bubbly tease,
Oh, what fun in the playful breeze!

The Air that Carries Stories

In the twist of winds, a tale unfurls,
Of sailors, mermaids, and treasure pearls.
A breeze that teases the passerby,
"Can you hear the sea's silly sigh?"

With every puff, a secret shared,
'Bout pirate socks and how none dared.
The salty air, a laugh in disguise,
Makes even crabs dance with surprise!

Whispers of dolphins in the swell,
Giggling stories that they tell.
They flick their tails in sheer delight,
As the sun dips low and teases night.

Each gust reminds, with every laugh,
Of the light-heartedness that they craft.
The air is filled with joyous schemes,
Blowing softly our wildest dreams!

Horizon's Anthem in Motion

As I stroll on shores where mariners tread,
I hear an anthem from waves instead.
Each lap of water, a chorus sings,
Of socks gone missing and seaweed rings!

The horizon winks with a playful stance,
Inviting clouds to join in a dance.
Oh, how they sway with rhythm so bright,
Bobbing and weaving 'til the night!

With every splash, the laughter echoes,
Tales of fish wearing pajama vests.
Comedic waves, they roll and tease,
As gulls roll their eyes in the gentle breeze.

Horizon's song, with a silly twist,
Makes clouds forget what shadows missed.
Boundless laughter in liquid form,
Where dreams and jesters both feel warm!

Fluttering Sailcloth and Spirits

Sails that flap like a laughing hand,
Catch the wind in a goofy stand.
They dance and twirl, oh what a sight!
As boats giggle and take flight!

A captain shouts with a grin so wide,
"Hold on, mates, let's enjoy the ride!"
With each gust, the spirits giggle,
Swaying the hulls, oh how they wiggle!

Flapping cloth, like kites in a race,
Spirits soaring in a playful chase.
The ocean swells as laughter swells,
Stories told in the bobbing bells!

As the sun dips low and colors bloom,
A grand finale to chase away gloom.
Fluttering sails in a joyous spree,
Whisper tales from the heart of the sea!

Embrace of the Nautical Air

The wind came in with a playful cheer,
Tugging at my hat, oh what a dear!
It twirled my snacks, danced my drink,
Made my shipmate spill, quick as a wink.

We laughed as seagulls swooped for fun,
Daring each other to run from the sun.
Fish in the waves seem to giggle too,
Waving their fins like a splashy crew.

Sun-kissed waves played tricks on the shore,
Find a laugh in a face of a bore.
The ocean's chuckle, a raucous spree,
Telling tales of mischief, wild and free.

So here we are, under skies so blue,
Chasing burbling breezes and that lovely view.
With every gust, we're in fits of glee,
As the wind whispers, "Come sail with me!"

Rhapsody of Nautical Whispers

Wind whispers softly, a secret delight,
Making the sailors take flight in the night.
A hat sails away on a rippling spree,
Chasing it down feels like pure jubilee.

Bubbles rise up from the depths below,
They burst with a giggle, a blubbery show!
Fish make remarks with a splashy snicker,
While I wait to see if my snack will flicker.

The sails flap hard, like a dance party's beat,
While gulls squawk out a tune so sweet.
Each gust is a prank, a frolicsome tease,
Turning calm waters to raucous unease.

We twirl and we whirl on this whimsical ride,
With waves as our partners, we slip and slide.
The salty air giggles in joyful spree,
And I'm lost in the laughter of the wind and the sea.

Breath of the Blue Horizon

Oh, the breezy breath of this ship afloat,
Whispers of mischief in the seagulls' coat.
It gently tugs on my sandwich so grand,
Sending it flying—how did it land?

The ocean grins like a wise old fool,
Where fish play cards in an underwater school.
Each wave paints a smile, each splash brings a cheer,
Every chuckling bubble, a raucous leer.

We ride the currents of laughter and waves,
While chasing the breezes that play like knaves.
The horizon beckons, a promise of play,
Oh, how I giggle at this watery ballet!

With every breeze comes a joke in disguise,
As I dance with the tides under bright sunny skies.
The air's full of whimsy, its charm hard to flee,
In this jolly embrace of the wide-open sea.

Melody of the Tempest's Caress

A tempest roars with a jovial laugh,
Throwing my boat a wild, wobbly path.
Waves pop like popcorn, all splashes and fun,
Oh, what a joyride under the sun!

The wind plays my hair like a fiddle so bright,
Twisting and twirling, what a silly sight!
Rain tickles my face, a wet slapstick play,
As I dodge flying hats that the tempest will sway.

Clouds giggle down from their lofty abode,
While pelicans sing in their watery code.
The sea sings a ditty, a rascal's refrain,
In the heart of the storm, it's all jokers and gain.

So let loose, wind friends, for we'll dance on this stage,
As the waves spin tales of our nautical rage.
With each gust we let out a blustery cheer,
For the joy of the tempest is forever near!

Dance of the Wind-Kissed Waves

The waves do jig, a splashy dance,
They wiggle and weave, given half a chance.
A seagull laughs, what a funny sight,
As seafoam twirls in the sun's bright light.

The flip-flops go flying, oh what a mess,
In the wind's embrace, no time to dress.
Sandcastles tumble, a sandy parade,
The tide's tickle brings a grand charade.

With laughter we skip, on the shoreline we play,
As the breeze tells jokes in its breezy way.
A crab joins in, shows off his best moves,
With jolly-old seaweed as he grooves.

So let's twirl like sea oats, under the sun,
With laughter and joy, we are all just as one.
The ocean's our stage, it's a hilarious feat,
Where every splash brings a giggly treat.

Echoes from the Salted Shore

Listen closely, what do you hear?
The surf's tickles, and a crab's loud cheer.
With shells as trumpets, the waves all play,
Making music that brightens our day.

A starfish croons with a wobbly tune,
While a seagull's clapping 'neath the bright moon.
The rocks are rolling, a band made of stone,
Under the sun's smile, we all feel at home.

The whispers of laughter ride on the waves,
As jellyfish joke through the briney caves.
In every splash, there's a hearty chuckle,
As the ocean puts on a merry knuckle.

So gather 'round the salted shore's realm,
Where nature's rhythms are eager to helm.
Each wave's a joker, with punchlines to spare,
Echoes of laughter float high in the air.

Serenade of the Tidal Winds

Come hither, my friends, let us roam,
Where breezes dance, and the waves call home.
Whispers of joy, on the salty breeze,
Invite us to twirl like a child in trees.

The wind makes faces, with a playful grin,
As shells roll by, laughing at kin.
A sea cucumber strums with great flair,
While mermaids giggle, tossing seashells in air.

With flippers and fins, the fish take a bow,
In this ocean ballet, here and now.
Their fins flicker jokes, with bubbles galore,
While crabs play the drums along the shore.

So let the tides sing, with laughter we sway,
To the serenade of fun, come what may.
In the salty air, we'll dance and spin,
With each joyful moment, let the fun begin!

Lullaby of the Coastal Zephyr

Oh sweet zephyr, with whispers so light,
You carry our giggles into the night.
Crickets play chess with the bustling sand,
While the moon chuckles, a wise, silver hand.

The tide gently nudges, "Come on, let's play!"
As starfish spin tales by the ocean's bay.
Fish in their tuxedos, all dressed for a ball,
Awaiting the tide's cue to leap and enthrall.

With a snicker and splash, the dolphins align,
Creating a splash that's simply divine.
Octopuses juggle, with arms all askew,
While the seaweed sways, just like we do.

So venture with me, on this wave-filled spree,
Where laughter and play are as wild as the sea.
In the lullaby's embrace, we find such delight,
As the coastal winds whisper us goodnight.

Swaying with the Seafoam

A feather floats, it's quite a sight,
Chasing down waves with all its might.
I tried to dance, but fell on my face,
That seafoam giggle, oh what a place!

Crabs are marching in a grand parade,
Snap at my toes, a feisty brigade.
They sidestep awkward, but oh so proud,
While I tumble over, falling aloud!

The seagulls squawk in a chorus grand,
As if to say, 'Come join our band!'
I wave my arms in a salty cheer,
Sliding on sand, with not a care here!

The tide rolls in, it tickles my feet,
A watery prank, oh life is sweet.
With laughter and waves, we take our stand,
In the shimmery froth, oh isn't it grand!

Breezes of Solitude and Reflection

A gentle puff brushes my cheek,
It whispers secrets, oh so unique.
Yet here I stand, a lone balloon,
Floating away, quite a silly tune!

It tugs at my hat, my hair in a whirl,
Wishing for calm while I twirl and twirl.
Oh breezy joker, you're quite the tease,
Dancing around like a playful breeze!

Shells giggle softly, a hidden crowd,
As I trip over laughter—oh how loud!
While pondering life like a clueless sage,
I'm the piñata in this salty page.

Yet solitude's charm isn't so grim,
With jokes from the waves and a whimsical whim.
Breezes of mirth, oh come take a ride,
In my heart, there's enough space inside!

Reach for the Distant Blue

I reached for the horizon, arms open wide,
But got tangled in kelp, oh what a ride!
The ocean laughs with its frothy waves,
Mocking my dreams of majestic saves!

Fish swim by with a curious glance,
While I do the cha-cha, caught in a trance.
A jellyfish floats by, looking confused,
And I think to myself, 'This is quite the muse!'

The sun peeks down, a jester in gold,
Casting funny shadows of tales yet untold.
I'll dance with the tides, share a laugh or two,
As I take in the beauty of the brilliant blue.

Artists paint scenes of this whimsical dance,
While I trip over shells in a goofy prance.
So here's to the ocean, the laughter it brings,
As I dream of mermaids with glittery wings!

Goddess of the Ocean's Caress

Oh goddess of waves, in a flip-flop race,
You pull me in with your tidal embrace.
But I stumble and slip on a tide-slick floor,
And laugh as I splatter—all dignity tore!

Your waves frolic with joy and delight,
While my hair develops a salty fright.
You tickle my toes, and I shriek with glee,
As I try to outpace such a slippery spree.

The sunbeams waltz on your shimmering back,
And I join in the fun, though I'm off the track.
Mermaids giggle, they know just what's true,
Life's funniest moments are served with a view!

With laughter and love, you caress the shore,
While I splish-splash about, asking for more.
So cheers to the goddess, with her playful caress,
In these waters of joy, I am truly blessed!

Kaleidoscope of Coastal Rhythms

The seagulls squawk in silly tunes,
As beach balls dance like cartoon balloons.
Sandcastles lean, a precarious sight,
With tourists' laughter echoing bright.

Waves roll in while flip-flops flee,
A crab does the cha-cha, wild and free.
Sunburned noses, a sight so grand,
As we toast with shells, beer in hand.

Kites soar high, they tangle and twist,
With kids screaming, "Look, I'm lost in mist!"
The ocean hums a jolly beat,
While sand tickles toes in a crazy feat.

So gather 'round, let's make a splash,
In coastal antics, we'll make a dash.
With giggles and sand in our hair,
Who needs the stress of daily care?

A Sip of Salty Freedom

A seagull swoops and steals my chip,
I laugh and shout, 'Hey, watch that slip!'
With salty air, I'm feeling bold,
As the ocean waves their tales unfold.

Barefoot strolls on the hot, warm sand,
A beach ball rolls - oh, isn't it grand?
Sunscreen mishaps, we smear and spread,
As laughter dances in our heads.

Here's to drinks topped with tiny umbrellas,
And making friends with silly fella.
Each wave that crashes, a goofy grin,
As we dive in, let the fun begin.

Oh, salty breeze, you tease and sway,
You steal my fries, yet here I play.
With each splash, we lift our cheer,
In tides of fun, we have no fear.

The Lure of the Wave's Kiss

A wave approaches with a sneaky giggle,
I jump to dodge, but it pulls my wiggle.
With sand in my snacks and salt in my hair,
Beach life is silly, without a care.

Waves break out in a ticklish ripple,
I tumble down like a clumsy dribble.
Friends by my side, we splash and cheer,
Our laughter dances across the pier.

Fishes swim by, making faces too,
They know the secret of fun in blue.
Each crash of the tide, a tickle delight,
As we run back to shore, hearts feeling light.

So here we stand, on the edge so free,
In this silly dance of wave and spree.
With sun hats flying, we chase the shore,
In moments of joy, who could ask for more?

Palette of Ocean Colors

The ocean wears shades of laughter and glee,
As umbrellas dance in hues of peach tea.
With splashes of giggles painted on sand,
A palette of joy, perfectly planned.

There's turquoise blue and coral red,
While jellyfish bounce on the ocean bed.
With flip-flops squeaking, we prance around,
While crabs in tuxedos struttin' abound.

The sun drops low, turning gold on the tide,
As we belly-flop in, our pride set aside.
With surfboards spinning and laughter galore,
We paint memories that we can't ignore.

So raise a toast to this canvas so wild,
With sea foam and sunshine, every adult is child.
In the rhythm of waves, we feel so bold,
In the palette of life, it's a sight to behold.

Embrace of the Coastal Zephyr

A gust of wind, a sunburned face,
I held my hat, what a wild chase!
It danced away like a playful sprite,
Laughing as it took off in flight.

The seagulls squawked, they joined the fun,
Diving for fries, oh what a run!
I shouted, "Hey, those are my chips!"
But they just flapped and did more flips.

Sand flew high like confetti tossed,
While I tried hard to dodge the frost.
A flip-flop flew past like a jet,
Uninvited guests I won't forget!

So here I sit, sandy and bright,
With a windy laugh, oh what a sight!
The zephyr knows how to stir things up,
With each puff, fills my heart like a cup.

Songs of the Windy Waters

Oh listen close, the waves they sing,
A melody of soggy bling!
They tickle toes and splash around,
The concert's loud, it won't back down!

A rogue wave soars, I squeal in glee,
As it sneaks up on my picnic spree.
My sandwich swims while seagulls cheer,
At this fine feast, oh what a year!

The ocean hums with jokes galore,
Tickling ears with a salty score.
I chuckle as my towel flies,
A puppet show beneath the skies!

A surfboard slips and then it falls,
While laughter echoes, the water calls.
We dance with joy, no care in sight,
Under the sun's warm, golden light.

Currents of Whispering Dreams

Whispers of tides, playful and sly,
They share secrets as they pass by.
"Hey, hold on tight!" the breezes tease,
As they swirl around with utmost ease.

Dreams of unicorns frolicking free,
Find their home in this salty spree.
The jellyfish jiggle, a wobbly sight,
As octopuses join in with delight.

A starfish grins, a five-armed smile,
As the sea turtle drifts for a while.
Living the life with a light-hearted cheer,
While the seagrass sways, with nothing to fear!

So here we play, in nature's spree,
Blown by currents, oh can't you see?
With every flicker, with every swirl,
I embrace these dreams, my ocean pearl.

Breezes That Invite

A breeze comes in, mischief unmasked,
Whispers of pranks, oh what a task!
It pulls my shirt, it twirls my hair,
Inviting all to join in the air.

With laughing gulls, oh what a crew,
They squawk at me, and swoop right through.
My drink's now a splash zone, full of fizz,
While the ocean smirks, with playful whizz!

The sun sets low, painting us bright,
As shadows dance, in the fading light.
While pinching crabs put on a show,
Tapping their claws, they steal the flow!

So come and join this crazy scene,
With breezes that flip every routine.
In this coastal whirl, we'll laugh and play,
As the breezy jesters steal the day!

Rhapsody of Distant Echoes

Whispers dance on salty air,
Seagulls gossip, unaware.
Clams wear shades, they sunbathe bright,
While fish do flip in sheer delight.

Sailboats tip and clang like bells,
Old sea dogs share their fishy tales.
A porpoise snickers, 'What a show!'
As jellyfish put on a glow.

Crabs arrange a crab rave party,
With dance moves that are quite hearty.
The tide comes in with a splish and flop,
As beach balls bounce and never stop.

In sandy shoes, we glide and slide,
While waves just giggle, and then they hide.
Oh, what fun this ocean spree,
Where every splash is pure comedy!

Language of the Open Waters

The ocean hums, a lively tune,
With surfboards chatting under the moon.
Starfish draw maps upon the shore,
While crabs hold meetings, 'What's in store?'

Shells whisper secrets of ancient quests,
As seaweed swaggers in its best jest.
A dolphin grins and says with glee,
'I hope you've got some fish for me!'

Bubbles rise with a pop and fizz,
Laughter rolls like waves, that's the biz.
In the surf, we dance like fools,
Chasing dreams in sandcastle schools.

The ocean's laughter fills the air,
A funny friend who's always there.
With every splash, a chuckle flows,
As jellyfish wear hats that glow!

Embrace of the Undulating Sea

Waves embrace with a cheeky grin,
Swirling around, let the fun begin.
Shells offer snacks, a tasty array,
As crabs take selfies, come what may.

Blowfish puff, then giggle loud,
At waves tall enough to feel proud.
The sunwarmed sand plays peek-a-boo,
While otters slide, splashing through the blue.

Seagulls dive with a squawky cheer,
Surfboards swirl in the salty sphere.
'Catch that wave!' is the call of choice,
And all join in with a silly voice.

At sunset, fish tell tales so grand,
Of treasure hunts in the golden sand.
With laughter echoing far and wide,
In ocean's arms, we take a ride!

Currents of Endless Longing

The tide pulls in with a playful nudge,
Fish play tag and the crabs all judge.
Octopuses flaunt with all their might,
While waves conspire to steal the light.

Seashells swap gossip, all in a swirl,
While tiny fish give a flirty twirl.
The moon grins down, a cheeky sprite,
As sailors laugh into the night.

A quirky squid juggles pearls with flair,
While dolphins practice aerial air.
The ocean's charm never seems to cease,
A comic stage that brings us peace.

With every splash, a hearty cheer,
In currents of laughter, we hold dear.
So come along, let's dip our toes,
Where the humor of the sea just grows!

Shadows of the Gale's Embrace

A seagull shouts, 'Hey, look at me!'
While dodging a kite, it makes quite a spree.
The fish flip-flop, in a splashy affair,
And the crabs throw a party in sun-drenched air.

Riding the waves, my hat takes a dive,
The wind giggles softly, like it's come alive.
With each gust, my map turns into confetti,
Directions? Who needs them? It's all quite heady!

Oceans of trouble, are they really there?
A flip-flop brigade is all I can wear!
With every hiccup, a giggle escapes,
The tide waves away all my dry, silly scrapes.

Laughter rolls in with the crashing foam,
Each wave whispers secrets, calling me home.
So here I float, on this whimsical ride,
With shadows and giggles all mixed with the tide.

Soliloquy of the Wandering Skiff

In my little boat, it's a wobbly dance,
I think I've found fish, but wait—just a chance!
The oars are my partners in shimmery play,
As seagulls sit judging, they yell, 'What a day!'

My compass, it spins like a top on the deck,
'North,' I insist, but it veers to the wreck.
Shall I search for treasure? Or just for a snack?
I row in circles; my sense is off track.

A friendly wave from a pirate with sass,
He stole my sandwich, but oh, I'll pass!
As the waves bubble up with hilarious drama,
Each laugh is a gem—now, where's my pajama?

With imagination as vast as the sea,
I'll anchor my dreams to the waves, wild and free.
Tomorrow I'll sail with the wind as my guide,
Ready for mischief—let the fun be my tide.

Breathless Moments at Waters' Edge

At the shoreline, the sand plays games with my toes,
A crab snaps a picture as laughter just grows.
The ocean's a jester, a slapstick display,
As I tumble and giggle, it sweeps me away.

A beach ball's flying, we all make a dive,
But wait! What's this? That splash—did I survive?
With dripping wet hair, it's a sight quite bizarre,
That beach towel's alive! Good times are the star.

Eruptions of giggles beneath a sun's gaze,
Seashells talk gossip of pleasant delays.
In flip-flops I dance, a tomfoolery trance,
While the tide rolls in with a whimsical prance.

So here on the shore, with the breeze laughing loud,
I'll chase all my worries, I'm feeling quite proud.
Each wave carries joy, as I frolic and sway,
Together we're laughing; let troubles decay.

Horizons Where the Sky Meets the Sea

Oh look at the horizon, a jellyfish glide,
It's moonwalking sideways, with stars as its guide.
The waves chant a tune, in a splishy-splash way,
I suspect they conspire for a silly ballet.

A dolphin in sunglasses shows off his best flip,
While a fish starts a conga—oh what a trip!
I cheer for my friends in this aquatic ball,
With each swirl and giggle, we're having a ball.

Clouds overhead giggle in fluffy parade,
While I throw out my worries; they drift like a trade.
The sun starts to whisper, 'Let's keep it absurd,'
And shadows shift shapes like they've just heard a word.

So let's sail towards laughter, where the sky winks back,
With humor as buoyancy, I won't feel the lack.
Each gust is a spark, each wave sings a song,
In the sea's lighthearted realm, we all belong.

Veil of the Ocean's Embrace

The ocean waves dance with glee,
As seagulls squawk a silly spree.
A crab wears shades, looking quite chic,
While dolphins giggle, just takes a peek.

The tide rolls in, with splashes bright,
Sandcastles topple, what a sight!
A fish in flip-flops flops away,
While beach umbrellas join the play.

There's laughter rolled up in the tide,
As waves chase shells that wish to hide.
With every breeze, the laughter flies,
The sea's a jester in disguise.

So grab your floaties, join the fun,
With fishy jokes, the day's begun.
In salted air, we all agree,
The ocean's heart beats wild and free.

Chime of the Seafoam Breeze

A whispering blast with a playful tease,
The ocean sings with a tickling breeze.
A jellyfish jives with dazzling flair,
While starfish giggle without a care.

Seagulls steal fries from picnics held,
As salty laughs in the air arepelled.
With every puff, the kites do sway,
Like underwater dancers in a ballet.

Sand in your shoes and a splashy splash,
A wave throws a party, come join the bash!
Frolicking fins and a crab doing flips,
The sea fizzles laughter, not just tips.

Let's dodge the waves, oh what a chase,
In this buoyant realm, we find our place.
With giggles carried on every breeze,
The ocean's tune is sure to please!

Tides of the Wandering Wind

The wind tells tales with a cheeky grin,
As kites take flight, let the fun begin.
A dolphin spins, a surfer falls,
While sandy feet make funny calls.

The seabreeze whispers, "What's that smell?"
"Oh dear, it's your socks, they've cast a spell!"
With giggling gulls and puffed-up cheeks,
The waves hold mischief, so to speak.

Paddleboard racers in a zany row,
Trying so hard, but oh, what a show!
With a flip or a flop, they splash about,
As seagulls squawk their raucous shout.

So grab your shades, let's hit the sand,
The breeze is calling, oh isn't it grand?
With laughter drifting through salty air,
Every moment's a joke, without a care.

Murmurs Along the Shoreline

The shoreline giggles with foamy waves,
As crabs do the cha-cha, oh how it raves!
A fish with glasses gives a wise wink,
While seaweed dances, in sync, in sync!

Shells gossip secrets, tossed by the tide,
While beachgoers trip, but take it in stride.
"Oops!" says the sand, with a cheeky grin,
As surfers tumble, laughter begins!

The ocean's voice is a playful song,
With whispers of joy that carry along.
From splashes and flops to sunburned glee,
The beach is a chuckle, come join the spree!

So, here's to the tales of the ocean's glee,
Where even the waves burst out with a knee.
With that salty breeze and merriment bright,
The laughter of shores beckons each night.

Dreamscapes on Salty Breezes

Beneath the sun, a seagull squawks,
Chasing chips, it secretly stalks.
With wings out wide, it swoops and dives,
While drivers laugh, their laughter thrives.

A crab in a hat, a sight to behold,
Shuffles sideways, a story untold.
It strikes a pose, like a grand film star,
While beachgoers watch from near and far.

Flip-flops flying, a dance in the sand,
Each salty breeze, a comedic band.
Kids chase the waves with squeals and glee,
As the tide takes their toys, oh whoopee!

The sun sets now, in hues so bright,
Squidward's cousins put up a fight.
With giggles and hats, they frolic like fools,
In dreamscapes of laughter, the ocean's cool rules.

Symphony of the Ocean Gale

The seagulls squawk with glee,
As waves dance wildly, you see.
A flip-flop flies, oh what a sight,
As I chase my hat in pure delight.

A crab sneaks up, he steals my fry,
I shout, 'Hey buddy, don't be shy!'
A dolphin laughs, flips in the air,
While I just sit, a salty stare.

The sand tickles my toes so free,
Like the jokes told by a sandy bee.
As foam erupts, I sing and twirl,
In this seaside fun, the waves unfurl.

Chasing Shadows on the Beach

I spot my shadow, oh so sly,
It runs away; I give a cry.
I dash through grains, my speed unmatched,
To catch that sneaky shape, I've latched.

A kid kicks sand, gets me all dirty,
A puff of laughter—now I'm flirty!
A wave comes crashing, sends me flying,
To seagulls cawing, 'He's just trying!'

A sandcastle falls, my trophy of fun,
While I chuckle with the setting sun.
With giggles echoing near the shore,
I'll chase my shadow forevermore.

Tides of Tranquility

The tide rolls in, a gentle tease,
As I sip lemonade with steady ease.
A beach ball bops, it floats my way,
I aim for it, but it saves the day!

My picnic spreads, but seagulls wail,
They dive with intent, a feathered trail.
I wave my sandwich, take a stand,
Yet all that's left is just some sand!

Sunshine glimmers, the fun won't cease,
As I build a sand fort; oh, what a piece!
With laughter shared as the sea breeze sighs,
Together, we dance where the ocean lies.

Wanderlust in Coastal Breezes

With a sip of soda, I feel alive,
My feet in the waves—come on, let's dive!
The beachcomber struts, a shell in hand,
But catches a crab—oh, isn't life grand?

The wind tousles hair as I twirl around,
While footprints get washed away, profound.
A sun tan lotion fight, oh what a scene,
As I slip on banana peels, I'm not so keen!

Yet laughter rings, my heart's in a rush,
I soak it in, relish in the hush.
Among the frolic, the sea's gentle tease,
There's joy in every fleeting breeze.

Whispers of Ocean Wind

A gull flew by with a cheeky squawk,
Wearing a hat made of driftwood stock.
The wind teased my hair, a wild curly fling,
As I strut like a penguin, oh what a thing!

It tickled my nose with a salty surprise,
As crabs played tag in their shell-bound disguise.
A beach ball escaped, rolled away with a cheer,
While I chased it down, puffing, filled with good cheer.

Oh, seaweed danced with a swaggering flair,
Making me wonder, does it really care?
With each gust that passes, I can't help but grin,
As the ocean keeps calling, "Come out and spin!"

The sand murmurs secrets, grains share a jest,
While I ponder whether to build or to rest.
The shoreline's a playground, can't you see?
As laughter and waves blend in crazy glee!

Dance of Salted Air

The breeze twirled 'round, a mischievous sprite,
Tried to steal my hat, oh what a sight!
It swooped and it swirled, then danced out of reach,
Leaving me giggling like a seagull at beach.

With fish in a line, on a hook they do wiggle,
While I trip on my flip-flops, oh, what a giggle!
The seafoam erupts with a frothy delight,
Tickling my toes, what a splashy respite!

A crab waved hello with a wobble so grand,
While the jellyfish jiggled, "Come join our band!"
The sun even chuckled, casting shadows galore,
As we pranced in the air, laughing more by the shore.

The waves rolled in rhythm, a silly parade,
Riding on foam, while my worries all fade.
And the salty embrace pulls me into its sway,
As the dance of the relaxed chases cares away!

Serenade of the Tidal Pull

The tide sings a tune with a splash and a roar,
As my beach chair collapses; I'm flat on the floor!
The sand in my sandwich gives crunch to my bite,
While the surf giggles softly, "We're all here for light!"

With seagulls as backup, they squawk out the beat,
As I juggle my snacks, but I can't find my seat.
In a drizzle of salt, I dance on my toes,
While sea turtles laugh at my awkward show.

The waves like a rhythm section, keep rolling along,
While I splash in the water, and sing out a song.
With clam shells for maracas, I join the wild rave,
As the sunset paints colors, a bright, silly wave.

So come on, my friends, let's frolic and twirl,
Make mischief with shells, give the waves a whirl!
For the life of a beach bum is the best kind of pull,
In the serenade sweet, we are all played the fool!

Echoes on the Shoreline

A conch shell whispers secrets of the sea,
While I try to interpret; it's baffling me!
With each grand wave crashing, I hear an old tune,
As I dance like a jellyfish, under the moon.

The sea invited me for an uproarious chat,
While crabs and dolphins wore bright party hats.
And every big splash was a laugh in disguise,
Making sure each giggle brought out silly cries.

The horizon grinned wide, painted orange and pink,
As I lost my cool cooler, it started to sink!
With a sea-swallowing burp, it flipped overboard,
And my snacks sailed away like a graceful accord.

So here let's all gather, by foam and by sun,
With laughter and smiles, we're having such fun!
Echoes on the shoreline will tickle the night,
As we dance with the wind, under stars shining bright!

Graceful Journeys in the Air

In puffy clouds, we spin and sway,
Birds giggle, 'Hey! Come join the play!'
Wind tickles noses, a frothy delight,
Laughter rides high, oh what a sight!

Mice surf the drafts on tiny boards,
Flying past trees, dodging the hordes.
Squirrels hold races, their tails in a whirl,
While bees do ballet, all around they twirl!

Up we go, chasing kites in the sun,
With every gust, adventure's begun.
Hold on tight, whimsical glee,
As we sail through the fun, you and me!

When the air gets silly, we dance with the breeze,
Birds make a fuss, passing peanuts with ease.
On this journey where laughter does soar,
Whimsical winds make us want even more!

Mellow Breezes of the Dusk

As day bows out, the breezes hum,
A playful tune with a quirky drum,
Fireflies waltz in the fading light,
While crickets chuckle in sheer delight.

The trees sway gently, sharing secrets bold,
About fluffy clouds and treasures of gold.
A brave little frog leaps high with flair,
Shouting, 'Catch me! If you dare!'

Whispers of laughter echo in the night,
While shadows play games, oh what a sight!
Stars peek down with a twinkle and tease,
As the world spins slowly with whimsical ease.

The wind carries tales from far and wide,
Of dogs in tuxedos, on barges they ride.
With each gust, a chuckle, a giggle, a cheer,
In the mellow dusk, joy is ever near!

Memento of the Ocean's Heart.

The waves dance high like a joyful choir,
Singing sweet songs that never tire.
Seagulls squawk jokes, perched up on beams,
While crabs share tales of their silly dreams.

The tide rolls in with a giggle and splash,
Making footprints and memories so rash.
A starfish winks, 'Look at my best pose!'
As jellyfish jiggle, wearing fancy clothes!

Buckets and shovels in hand, we dig,
Building grand castles, all dressed like a twig.
'Beware the tide!' we hear someone say,
But laughter takes over– let's play all day!

In seashell whispers and salty mists,
Fun's in the air, and no joy is missed.
With each splash and ripple, watch the sun smart,
Seashells collect laughter, they echo the heart!

Whispers of the Ocean's Breath

The ocean chuckles as waves come and go,
Sprinkling giggles in a frothy show.
Sandcastles tumble, but who really cares?
When mermaids are laughing, combing their hairs!

The breeze carries secrets from shipmates abroad,
And tales of lost treasures that leave us awed.
Octopuses juggle with seashells in hand,
While dolphins hold parties in their underwater band!

Bubbles of laughter float high in the air,
Making fish blush, with their scales laid bare.
A sea cucumber whispers a secret so sly,
While crabs take a bow, 'We were born to fly!'

As night draws close with its galactic art,
The sea takes a breath, a pause to restart.
With every wave's giggle, connection we find,
In whispers and tickles, the ocean's aligned!

Harmonies in the Salt Air

The seagulls scream, a cheeky cheer,
They plunder chips without a fear.
With waves that crash and bubbles burst,
We laugh so hard, our stomachs thirst.

The salty breeze, it plays a tune,
It tickles noses, makes us swoon.
With every gust, our hats take flight,
A comical dance in broad daylight.

Sunburned backs and sandy toes,
Each summer day, a laugh that flows.
The tide rolls in, the fun begun,
Beneath the sun, we're all just one.

So join the song, the frothy glee,
In every breeze, we're wild and free.
The shore's our stage, let's be the jest,
For laughter's the true sailor's quest.

Romance of the Wandering Wind

Oh, how he woos, that flirty breeze,
With tousled hair and spirits free.
He swoops past beach towels and cold drinks,
Just to tease, oh how he thinks!

He tosses hats and twirls the flags,
Chasing after the fishermen's rags.
With a playful wink and a swirl of zest,
He charms the boats, they feel so blessed.

But don't be fooled, he's here for fun,
A whirlwind romance that's never done.
With every gust, he breaks the chain,
A flirtatious breeze, never mundane.

So here's to winds that love to play,
Whispering secrets in a silly way.
In ocean's breath, love's laughter sings,
A playful breeze with vibrant wings.

Untold Stories of the Shore

Listen closely, the tides have tales,
Of crabby crabs and wind-blown sails.
A beach ball lost in a hasty tide,
It's still afloat, that silly ride!

The starfish grins, a lopsided joy,
While clams perform, their pearl deploy.
The waves tell jokes, just out of ear,
Each splash a chuckle, a friendly cheer.

We gather shells that joke and tease,
Each one a story, sure to please.
With laughter ringing on the sand,
The shore's a circus, oh so grand!

So let's collect these tales so dear,
From dancing crabs to waves that cheer.
In every grain, a giggle stored,
The shore's a place where we're adored.

Echoes of Adventure

With every wave, a guffaw rings,
As paddles splash and laughter sings.
The surfboards wobble, here we go,
Oops, down I plunge, a splishy show!

A jellyfish winks, it's quite the prank,
While kids run wild, their courage frank.
The tide's our guide, a cheeky mate,
Encouraging dives, it's never late.

A kite takes flight, a frantic chase,
As giggles spill upon the face.
With childhood dreams in salty air,
Each echoed laugh a vibrant flare.

So come along, let's ride the wave,
Adventure calls, be bold and brave.
For in these echoes, joy abounds,
In laughter's symphony, life resounds.

Songs of the Twilight Tide

The wind tickles my ear, oh what a jest,
With sea foam laughter, I can't help but jest.
Seagulls performing a dance on the waves,
Rumors of treasure, they say, it behaves!

Jellyfish float by like bobbing balloons,
Quarrels between crabs, oh their silly tunes.
A fish in a tux with a top hat so grand,
Waving his fin like a pompous bandstand.

Whispers of mermaids, they giggle and splash,
With shells as their hats, oh what a fine clash!
The ocean's so quirky, I'm losing my mind,
Sandy shoes and all, let's leave cares behind.

As twilight descends, the fun doesn't cease,
We dance with the waves, a whimsical lease.
So here I will stay, with a smile and a cheer,
For night brings its jokes, and the sea sings them near.

Emissaries of the Wind's Whisper

The breeze has a mustache, it tickles my nose,
With tales of the briny, where no one quite knows.
A crab wearing goggles shouts, 'Look at me!'
While fish in a chorus hum, 'We're fancy and free!'

Driftwood with secrets, each twist tells a tale,
Of sailors who danced with their feet in a gale.
Seagulls compete for the best fishy prize,
With cheers and their caws, they're true ocean spies.

The tide's like a laugh, it ebbs and it flows,
Tugging at toes, oh where did it go?
Surfboards like whales, they flop left and right,
As giggles erupt in the soft moonlight.

With whispers of wind and sun's cheeky waves,
We chase down our dreams like colorful knaves.
The sea friends unite in a bubble of glee,
As laughter rides high on the back of the sea.

Mosaic of the Ocean's Breath

Each wave carries secrets, a playful delight,
With laughter as riches, the moon's shining bright.
A sea snail in boots struts along with great flair,
While starfish debate if life's fair or unfair.

The ocean dreams up a festival sound,
Where bubbles and giggles are happily found.
A dolphin in shades is the life of the bash,
While everyone marvels at his epic splash.

With shells as our trophies, we decorate sand,
A parade of sea creatures, so lively and grand.
I'd trade my old shoes for a fishtail or two,
And join in the fun, oh what mischief to pursue!

Twinkling lights shimmer on that swaying floor,
As jellyfish glide by with a curious roar.
In this mosaic of joy, we dance through the night,
With smiles as our markers, everything feels right.

Journey of the Wind-Woven Talks

The breeze comes on strong with its rambunctious charm,

It teases the gulls, causing heads to disarm.
A clam with a frown holds a not-so-great court,
Judging the antics of beach toys on sport.

Laughter bounces along like a beach ball in flight,
With surfboards that wobble, they're quite the sight!
A hermit crab scurries, his house is too small,
In search of a mansion, he makes quite the call.

Sandcastles crumbling, we cheer for their fate,
As waves sneak around for their well-timed date.
The ocean's alive with the giggles and shouts,
As we gather around for our silly, loud bouts.

So here's to the winds and their chatter so bright,
With seaweed confetti, we dance through the night.
In this warm ocean party, we're all having fun,
For each silly moment makes the journey well done!

www.ingramcontent.com/pod-product-compliance
Lightning Source LLC
Chambersburg PA
CBHW072223070526
44585CB00015B/1467